RADSPORTS GUIDES

BMX FREESTYLE

TRACY NELSON MAURER

Rourke Publishing LLC
Vero Beach, Florida 32964

www.rourkepublishing.com

Project Assistance:
Jeremy Bellamy and the staff of Stewart's Bikes & Sports in Duluth, MN, and the staff of Superior Sports in Superior, WI, generously shared their expertise.

Also, the author extends appreciation to Mike Maurer, Kendall and Lois M. Nelson, Harlan Maurer, and Drs. Steven Massopust, Timothy Rich and Boyd Erdman.

Photo Credits:
Page 4: © Tom Hauck/Allsport; page 7: © Jon Ferrey/Allsport; pages 8 and 10: © Donald Miralle/Allsport; page 11: © Simon Bruty/Allsport; page 13 and 23: © Jamie Squire/Allsport; page 14: © Jed Jacobsohn/Allsport; page 16: © ECS; page 23; page 27: © Todd Warshaw/Allsport

Editorial Services:
Pamela Schroeder

Notice: This book contains information that is true, complete and accurate to the best of our knowledge. However, the author and Rourke Publishing LLC offer all recommendations and suggestions without any guarantees and disclaim all liability incurred in connection with the use of this information.

Safety first! Activities appearing or described in this publication may be dangerous. Always wear safety gear. Even with complete safety gear, risk of injury still exists.

Library of Congress Cataloging-in-Publication Data

Maurer, Tracy Nelson
    BMX Freestyle / Tracy Nelson Maurer
      p. cm — (Radsports guides)
    Includes bibliographical references and index.
    Summary: Surveys the history, equipment, techniques, and safety factors of freestyle cross-country bicycle racing.
    ISBN 1-58952-102-1
    1. Bicycle motocross—Juvenile literature. [1. Bicycle motocross.] I. Title

GV1049.3 .M38 2001
796.6'2—dc21   2002041655

Printed in the USA

TABLE OF CONTENTS

Fast-paced BMX racing challenges riders all over the world.

DIRTY, FAST, AND WILD

BMX bicycles cover a lot of ground, from dirt tracks to cement skate parks. You see these small-wheeled bikes everywhere. They rip down streets in cities and small towns across America. They charge over Europe's avenues. They bump across the Australian outback. All over the world, BMX attracts riders from age 6 to well past age 60. That's not bad for a sport that began as a copycat.

chapter
ONE

BMX took its name from motorcycle's cross-country racing, called motocross or MX. Ten years later, bicyclists copying the motorized racers started calling their sprints "bicycle motocross." They used the letters "BMX." The name stuck.

BMX BREAKS OUT

BMX blasted off in the 1970s with the Sting Ray model from the Schwinn Bicycle Company. This first popular BMX bike used a swooped seat and knobby, dirt-hugging tires. It looked fast and fun, and it delivered.

Kids flew around empty swimming pools, pounded dirt trails, jumped dirt hills, and dropped into the ramps at newly opened skate parks. Indoor and outdoor racecourses opened, often hosting more than 50 races in a day.

Soon other sports stole the limelight and BMX lost some steam. A surge again in the 1980s brought out new bike designs that improved speed and allowed more stunts. Still, BMX lagged behind the other action sports. Its loyal but few riders lived mainly in warm-weather states, such as California and Florida.

Then the ESPN X Games in the 1990s broke open a BMX bonanza with high-flying tricks, racing, and other contests. The small, one-speed bikes finally shook off the fad label.

When did the BMX bug bite you?

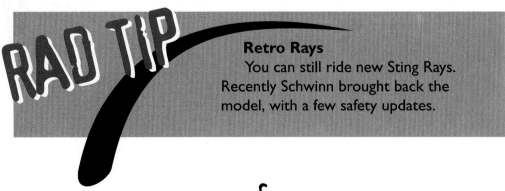

RAD TIP

Retro Rays
You can still ride new Sting Rays. Recently Schwinn brought back the model, with a few safety updates.

Advanced BMX freestyle riders try to catch big air for awesome tricks.

BMX racers practice by riding on a track or on dirt paths.

ROOTS IN RACING

BMX riding once meant dirt, speed, and more speed. Every 20" bike had knobby tires and a checkered-flag mission. Racing ruled. Today you can choose from two types of BMX riding styles: racing and freestyle. You can cross between them if you just want to ride for fun. Advanced riders usually stick to one area.

Although freestyle catches the TV cameras these days, BMX racing attracts riders and fans worldwide. It's fairly easy to start racing, whether you're a girl or boy. You race against other riders of the same age and sex. Beginners, novices, and experts run separate races. Strict safety rules help earn the parental stamp of approval, too. In fact, fewer kids hurt themselves in BMX races than they do in soccer matches.

An inspector checks your bike before the race to make sure it won't hurt you or anyone else. One raw edge can make mincemeat out of a pile-up. Every rider must wear a helmet, usually a full-face helmet. Check your track's rules before you show up on race day.

RACE DAY STRATEGY

Walk the track to decide your **strategy** on race day. Plan how to handle the banked corners, or berms. Check out how the racers line up. Eight at a time nose their front wheels against an upright plank. They take their starts very seriously. They pounce on the pedals when the plank drops and shoot down the slight ramp onto the course. Usually the racer who nails the holeshot, or leading position, from the starting gate wins the race.

A lot of riders crash or "endo" in the first rush out of the gate. Those who jostle through the pack quickly reach 30 mph (18.75 kph). They rip their lines across the berm and rattle across "whoops," or tightly spaced bumps. Then they fly off a tabletop jump toward the finish line. The race ends in about 30 seconds. That's fast fun!

Endos often happen when the pack of bikes busts out from the starting plank.

This rider knows to keep her pedals up on the berm, or sloped corner.

TRACK DOWN A TRACK

Hundreds of tracks hold motos, or bracket races, in the United States. Your local bike shop can help you find a track nearby. Check on the Internet, too. The American Bicycle Association (ABA), reigning on the West Coast, and the National Bicycle League (NBL), ruling on the East Coast, can point you in the right direction.

The ABA and NBL also host dirt jumping contests, even though jumping usually means freestyle. Some people start racing for the jumps, not the speed. Sure, that muddies up the picture a bit. But if you want clean, ride your washing machine and forget BMX.

FREESTYLE TAKES OFF

Freestyle BMX focuses on stunts or tricks. You ride alone on your bike and do the tricks you like to do. You do them your way. You can even make up your own moves and give them names. Creative and **independent** riders usually lean toward the freestyle **disciplines**—dirt jumping, mini/park, vert, street, or flatland.

Speed   ★★★★★
Big air   ★★★★★
Tricks   ★★★★★
Technical ★★

1. Dirt jumping

Dirt jumping started with motorcycles, and BMX riders learned from them. Many of the tricks share the same names, like the Superman (gliding through the air in a stretched-out position, holding on by the handlebars). Bulldozers and Bobcats carve out mounds of earth for takeoff ramps and landing ramps. You pedal like a banshee to catch big air. You throw a trick and try to land on the ramp, touching down with the rear wheel first. Some jumpers just go for distance. They may opt for metal ramps to leap over cars and other handy **obstacles**.

Speed   ★★★
Big air   ★★★
Tricks   ★★★★★
Technical ★★★

2. Mini/Park

Riding in skate parks or on mini-ramps gives you new ways to move your bike. Smooth **terrain** and sharp angles on ramps change the way you set up tricks. Most parks have beams you can grind, or slide, your bike on. It's not harder, but it's different. You see small-air moves and more technical tricks off the mini-ramps. Watch the more advanced riders for clues about the ramps to hit in the park. Skate parks avoid traffic and other road dangers, and they bring a lot of different riders together. You learn faster from the experienced riders. Too many riders at one time clog up the park; take turns and shred peacefully.

*Small movements, like pushing your shin into the top tube,
can help smooth out your tricks.*

Even simple vert tricks take time to master. Always wear your safety gear in the half-pipe.

Speed   ★★★
Big Air   ★★★★★
Tricks   ★★★★★
Technical ★★★

3. Vert

Vert, or half-pipe, tricks look awesome and camera guys swarm all over the skate parks to catch the action. "Vert" comes from the vertical walls on each side of the U-shaped half-pipe ramp. If the walls *angled* outward, the riders would launch next door. Although you usually see half-pipes in a skate park, not all BMX riders at the park dare to drop into the U-ramps. It's mainly the hard-core BMX riders jamming there. They catch 12 feet (3.7 m) of oxygen straight up from the half-pipe wall. That's big air. They pull major tricks while they're airborne. It's not the place for beginners. Those verts can **intimidate** even experienced riders.

Speed   ★★★★
Big Air   ★★
Tricks   ★★★★
Technical ★★★

4. Street

True street riding is just that—riding in the streets, hitting tricks wherever you find them. Street riders grind and jump using ledges, stair handrails, benches, curbs, walls, gaps between buildings and other urban obstacles. The danger level ranks high and beginners should stick close to home. Also, property owners usually don't leave out a welcome mat. Some cities issue tickets to riders. These aren't the "street" competitions you see on TV with their perfectly spaced gaps, smooth rails, and specially-designed ramps.

Remember to start with simple tricks. Mastering the easier tricks first can save you embarrassment and possibly hospital time.

Speed   ★★
Big air   ★★
Tricks   ★★★★★
Technical   ★★★★★

5. Flatland

Some people say flatland riding looks like dancing with a bike. Timing, rhythm, and balance set these tricks apart from the gutsy airborne shows. Parking lots and other flat, smooth surfaces work well for flatland tricks. Even new riders can do basic flatlander moves. But most of the tricks require **precision** and skill. Professional flatlanders practice six to ten hours a day.

FINDING YOUR RIDE

Your bike says a lot about you. In a flash, other riders know if you're a "real rider" or a poser. Posers don't practice much (if ever), but they whine because they don't know many tricks. They ride sweet bikes and act like they're cool. A fancy bike means nothing in freestyle BMX, unless you really ride it.

Real riders love the sport. They ride for the fun of it. They ride as much as they can on any bike they can keep cobbled together. They do as many tricks as they can. They ride flatland, street, vert, park, jumps and ramps. They try it all. Then they try harder. Now you know how to ride like a pro.

chapter

TWO

SHOP WISELY

If you know that you don't have the strength, skills, or the guts to do tricks, then try a discount-store bike. They start around $100. These bikes ride just fine on the street. Take them out for jumps, grinds, or other tricks if you want, but bring along a box to carry home the pieces.

The quality, strength, and performance rises with the price. Entry-level bikes at a bike shop start around $250. What you save at first on a discount bike, you spend later for replacement parts, repair fees, and hospital bills.

DECISIONS, DECISIONS, DECISIONS

A good bike shop salesperson asks you what you want to do with your bike before showing you any kind of model. Be honest. Bike manufacturers offer models that cater to every style of riding at every skill level. You can ride the same bike for flatland, street, vert, or dirt jumping. Some bike designs simply perform better in one discipline than another.

In general, a racing BMX bike uses an aluminum frame to make it lightweight. A freestyle BMX bike weighs a bit more than a racer for added stability and durability. Tricks beat on a bike. Dirt jumping pounds on bikes. Jumping BMX bikes use the beefiest frames of all to handle the abuse. Think of jump bikes as tanks on two wheels with invisible wings.

Mostly, you need a bike that feels right. Test drive a few at the bike shop. Ride your friends' bikes. Read BMX magazines and surf websites until you understand the different designs.

READY TO RIDE

New riders usually buy their first bikes whole—no assembly required. Nearly all freestyle BMX bikes come with:

- One-speed pedal power
- No kickstand
- A cable detangler
- **Traction** spikes on the pedals
- Four metal pegs on the axles
- Front and back caliper brakes

You can replace and upgrade any part of the bike. Advanced riders often piece theirs together with specific parts from different manufacturers. Building a bike from scratch easily doubles the cost.

RAD TIP

Used ... And Abused?
You can save a few bucks buying a used bike. Ask the bike shop for trade-ins, watch the want ads in your paper or surf the Net. Once you find a bike, check the frame and joints with a magnifying glass. Any cracks mean trouble. Brakes should work well and the rims should look straight.

KNOW YOUR PARTS & PIECES

Know the bike's parts. Many tricks use specific parts of the bike. For example, a "nosepick" means stalling on your front tire. An "icepick" means stalling on a rear peg. A "toothpick" means stalling on a front peg.

Frame – The metal tubing that supports the bike and is often welded in the shape of triangles. Brazing welds create stronger metal joints than traditional welds.

Front Fork – A sturdy rod that splits into two legs. At the ends of the legs, slots called dropouts hold the front wheel axles. The fork angles outward to add steering control.

Handlebars – Two curved bars set into the headset tube at the neck of the bike. Position your bars so you don't stretch to reach them. But don't knock your knees on them either. Soft rubber grips on the handlebars add control and cover any ragged metal. Notice the lack of pom-poms, please.

Saddle – This is the seat. Racers and basic freestyle bikes come with lightweight and rock-hard plastic saddles. You don't sit down much, so this isn't a big deal. Some better bikes offer cushioned saddles—again, not a big deal.

Pegs – Four metal tubes sticking out each side of the front and rear axles. Sized like toilet-paper tubes, pegs let you amp up your tricks. Look for steel pegs (unless you just want them for show).

Wheels – Two round devices that spin when you pedal. Most BMX bikes use 20" diameter wheels. You measure from outside of the tire across to the other outside. Fine metal spokes connect the center hub to the rim. This reduces wobble. Mag wheels look cool.

Tires – The black, flexible tubing around the wheels. For years, you saw only deep-treaded knobbies on BMX tires. Chunky knobbies still exist. You also see flatter swirls and other patterns that stick better to ramps, asphalt, and cement.

Pedals – Two thin blocks sticking out from the cranks, one on each side of your bike. Basic bikes use plastic pedals. Serious bikes use alloy or metal pedals. Small studs hold your feet on. Toe clips would drag you down.

Cranks – Two metal shafts attached to the pedals and the drive train. BMX cranks, longer than regular bike cranks, deliver more power and speed. Some bikes use one-piece cranks. Pro bikes use three-piece bolted cranks.

Drive Train – The section of bike that includes the pedals, cranks, chainwheel (front sprocket), and cog or freewheel (rear sprocket). This system changes your vertical, or up and down, movement into horizontal, or forward movement. Most bikes put the drive train on the right where most riders push the hardest. Some companies make left-side drive options now. Depending on how you ride, this may reduce drive-train thrashings.

Brakes – A hand-operated stopping system. Cables pull on U-shaped metal **calipers** to put pressure on both sides of the front and rear rims. A cable detangler by the headset lets you spin the handlebars 360°. Some racing BMX bikes use a linear pole brake for faster stopping. They skip the front brake.

Safety Pads – The cushions wrapped around the frame, stem, and handlebars on racing bikes. Rare in freestyle.

CHECK IT OVER

Real BMX bikes show the fine results of mixing **physics** and fun. Treat your bike well and you'll go further with it. Read your owner's manual. It actually contains useful information, especially about caring for your machine. **Lubricate** the chain and cables as directed. Ask your bike shop to recommend a dry spray (it's usually on the checkout counter).

As you ride, listen for odd noises. Find out what's making them (beans for dinner doesn't count). Clean your bike after every ride. Spraying it with a hose is lame. Wipe with a soft, damp rag. Look for any cracks in the frame while you're so close to it.

Just like a car, your bike needs regular tune-ups. Unless you really, really, really know what you're doing, visit the masters in the bike shop.

RAD TIP

Tool Kit Corner
You can buy bike maintenance tools for about $50-$100. Before you plunk down the big bucks, pick up the basics: tire hand-pump, tire pressure gauge, cleaning supplies, bike lubricant, and spoke wrench.

Ask for maintenance advice from your local bike shop.

YOUR BIKE-CARE CHECK LIST

Write down a check list. Use this one as a guide and add any other tips from your handy-dandy owner's manual. Tape it to your garage wall. Date it every time you do it.

1. **Handlebars** — Test for wobble. Tighten the head bolt on top of the stem.

2. **Tires** — At least once a week, use a tire gauge to check for the correct psi (pounds per square inch), stamped on the side of each tire. Gas station air hoses blow up a tire very easily—"blow up" as in explode with an amazingly loud *whaaapp* sound. Use a hand pump instead.

3. **Wheels** — Set the bike upside down on the handlebars and seat. Spin the front wheel to check for wobble, which could mean a bent rim or worn bearings. Also tweak each spoke. A "ping" sound is good. A "tunk" sound is loose. Turn a loose spoke about a quarter or half turn with a spoke wrench (about $5). Crank the pedals to check the rear wheel the same way.

4. **Chain** — Press it down with your thumb. You should see about 1/2 inch (1.3 cm) of give. If it's too loose, the chain could jump off the sprocket. Too tight, and it could snap.

5. **Brakes** — Heavy use stretches the cables. Tighten them according to the owner's manual.

SAFE RIDING

Freestylers need more gear than a bike and some tools. Think about what you wear, too. The more skin you cover, the less you can crayon, or skid, across the pavement and dirt.

You don't have to dress like a sports freak. Your favorite long-sleeve T-shirt, baggy shorts, and flat-bottom sneakers, especially high-tops, work just fine for freestyle.

Forget the baggy jeans, though. Your chain eats them like candy. You can buy cuff clips or borrow your dad's (yeah, right).

chapter

THREE

BEYOND THE BIKE

Try on a few helmets at the bike shop. You want the helmet to fit snugly. Look for the safety seal on it, too.

Half-cut, or open-face, helmets usually feel lighter and more comfortable than the full-face versions. They also cost about half as much. Before you buy one, however, ask yourself how much your face and teeth are worth to you. Most full-face helmets cost less than an **emergency** room visit.

Wear your helmet. Most kids do, so you won't get laughed at. Plus, most skate parks and racecourses require brain buckets. Woodward Camp, the most famous BMX riding center in America, requires every biker to wear a helmet. They recommend full-face helmets for vert and trail riding.

MORE BODY ARMOR

Woodward and most other skate facilities also require knee pads, elbow pads, shin guards, and gloves. Some kids hide the padding under their clothes, but they still wear them.

Racers wear long-sleeve jerseys and pants, called leathers, made of heavy-duty nylon and built-in padding. This "armor" protects knees, hips, and shins.

Even flatlanders and street riders wear gloves. Sweat and heat can make the handlebar grips slippery. Gloves, either in full-finger or fingerless styles, also prevent blisters and scrapes.

HELMET

ELBOW PADS

JERSEY

GLOVES

KNEE PADS

SHIN GUARDS

PERFORMANCE SHOES

Try not to stick out your hands or legs when you crash.

HIT THE DIRT

Everybody hits the dirt. Bruises, scrapes and scabs look like badges of honor on BMX riders. Road rash looks nasty but heals quickly. Wash it as soon as you can. Put on an **antiseptic** cream or spray, and let the wound heal without a bandage.

Three tips on road rash:

1. Don't cover road rash unless it looks too gross for public display.
2. See a doctor if you can't clean out the wound or it looks too deep and meaty for ordinary bandages.
3. If the scab feels crusty and stiff, apply a thin layer of **petroleum** jelly to keep it from cracking when you ride.

You should also seek medical attention if you whack your head hard enough to see stars. If your vision is cloudy, you feel stabbing pains, or you think you broke something, ask someone to bring you to the emergency center.

RAD TIP

Road Rash Stash
For all-day riding, carry a water bottle and a stash pack filled with basic first-aid supplies. Include a few large bandages, gauze pads, antiseptic wipes, and antiseptic ointment.

BREAK FALLS, NOT BONES

Wearing your safety gear prevents many injuries. Still, practicing stunts is risky. Among ages 10 to 14, the most common injuries include **fractures**, strains and sprains to the arms, hands, wrists and lower legs.

Knowing how to fall reduces your hospital visits. Don't stick out your hands or feet to break your fall. High-impact landings often snap arm and leg bones. When you crash, stay relaxed. Drop onto a shoulder with your arms covering your face or near your head. Tuck in your chin and roll across your back with your knees bent up. Spread the impact across your upper body.

LICENSE THAT VEHICLE

Many city laws require that you license your bike. The police ask for the serial number (found under the frame by the pedals). If they find your bike after it was lost or stolen, they will trace it by the serial number to return it to you.

Also, buy a lock. Use it. Put it around your rear wheel and the frame. Then connect it to a **stationary** object, like a cemented lamp post. U-locks use a round key system that a thief can't pick easily. Hacking at it takes too much time for most slackers.

RIDE ON THE RIGHT SIDE OF THE LAW

Bikes qualify as wheeled vehicles. You must obey traffic laws when you ride. Stop at stop signs. Signal your turns. Ride on the right. Pass on the left. Yield to walkers, joggers, and any other **pedestrians**.

The police give motorcycle and vehicle drivers tickets for wearing headphones. In most places, you can wear them on your bike legally, but it's not a good idea. Headphones can distract you from riding safely. Cranking up the volume louder than a car horn (40 decibels) may cause deafness. Some cities also ticket you for it.

Also the law says bicycles must have **reflectors** when they leave the store. Keep your reflectors on. Don't ever ride your bike at night without a light ahead of you and one behind you. A black bear at midnight is easier to see than an unlit bike.

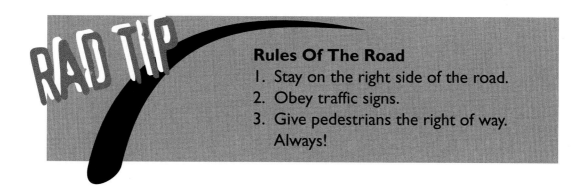

RAD TIP

Rules Of The Road
1. Stay on the right side of the road.
2. Obey traffic signs.
3. Give pedestrians the right of way. Always!

Sharing space at a local skate park is often not a problem.
Just keep your speed in check and ride with caution.

READY, SET, GO

If you're new on a BMX bike, look for an open lot with soft dirt for practicing. Crashing on the ground instead of cement or asphalt cushions your fall. A normal bike responds slower than a BMX bike. You might need to adjust how you ride on the BMX. Check that the ball of your foot centers on the pedal. Practice turning with speed. Dab, or put a foot down only when you lean too far over. Remember to keep the inside pedal up when you come around a corner. Then practice stopping. If you rode a coaster-brake bike before, using your hands to squeeze the brakes feels goofy at first.

RIDE IN PEACE

Some advanced freestyle riders cruise the city streets looking for places to try tricks. Not every campus, business, or urban center allows bikes. Many BMX riders have police records for riding in banned areas. Fines and tickets add up. Ride right.

Many better riders look for a change of pace at their local skate parks. Don't expect a happy greeting. American parks tend to separate the two-wheelers from the four-wheelers or ban bikes completely. Some city officials believe bikes ruin the park surfaces. However, properly built parks withstand just about any thrashing from bikes, blades (in-line skates), and boards (skateboards)—called the B3s or three Bs.

A few officials argue that bikers plow over the kids on boards and in-line skates. History shows bikes and boards can roll safely together. All European public parks allow the three Bs without trouble.

Help skate parks work better for all shredders. Drop the cocky attitude. Instead, take turns in the park. Wait until other riders clear a ramp before you try to use it. Don't hog the ramps. Take just one run during your turn. That means if you fall, stop, jump off, or miss a trick, then move out of the way for the next person.

Use common sense. Ride with **courtesy**. Everyone has more fun.

RAD TIP

Quick Fix Trick

Wherever you ride, you might need a quick fix. Tape a spare chain link onto your saddle rails. Carry a spare inner tube, chain link, plastic cable ties and a Leatherman-style heavy-duty multi-purpose tool in your stash pack.

TRICKS

Freestyle tricks look easy when they're done right. Those smooth moves take a lot of practice, plus a few bumps and bruises along the way, too. Some professional riders spend six to ten hours every day trying new tricks and dialing in their favorites.

Patience and practice take you from the basics to the big-time moves.

chapter
FOUR

Check on the Internet and talk to experienced riders for tips before you try new tricks. Many of the moves twist the laws of physics. Watch tricks closely to see if you should:

- Stand or sit?
- Shift your weight forward, or back, or center?
- Hold the handlebar grips? If not, then where do the hands go?
- Put your feet on the pedals? If not, then where do the feet go?
- Keep the pedals level? Right pedal up? Left pedal up?
- Lead with your head? For spins, your head begins the turning motion.

BASIC TRICKS

Where you ride tends to decide which tricks you learn. If you ride in a skate park, you will focus more on ramp work, for example. The differences in tricks become greater as you improve. Pro flatlanders practice far different moves than pro vert riders. Some books and websites separate their tricks according to riding style. Don't limit yourself to one style—you might miss out on something fun! Every BMX freestyler learns these tricks before moving up to advanced moves.

1. **Bunny-hop** – At a medium speed, you lift both wheels off the ground. Sounds simple enough, but it takes time before you can hop high enough to land on a curb or rail. Dial in this trick. You need it for many others. For example, you bunny-hop to put your front wheel and back peg onto a ledge for a feeble grind.

2. **Curb endo** – This is a front-wheel wheelie. Endo, short for end-over-end, requires speed control. Too fast and you endo right over the curb. Sit down, ride slowly, and aim for a curb or ledge. Level your pedals. Just as the wheel touches the curb, quickly stand up and push forward on the handlebars. Bend your knees as the rear wheel rises.

3. **Wheelie** – Pedaling at a medium speed, move your weight back toward the rear wheel and pull up on the handlebars. Repeat. Repeat. Repeat. Hold it longer every time. Similar to a wheelie, a manual works without the pedals. The trick? Tap your brakes to help keep your balance when you feel like you're tipping backwards.

4. **180 (say: one-eighty) Barspin** – If you're right-handed, roll slowly counterclockwise in a large circle. (Left-handers should switch these instructions for the opposite side.) Reach under for the left grip with your right hand. Whip the bars 180°, or half-way around. Keep the pedals level. Spread your knees apart so they clear the bars. Repeat to bring the handlebars back around. When you nail the 180, start working on a 360—or full circle. Gawkers love to see barspins!

RAD TIP

Practice the feel of an endo position by asking a buddy to hold your rear wheel in the air. Use the brakes to hold yourself in position.

BIG AIR STARTS SMALL

Use a small bump or ramp for building your jumping skills. Pedal fast until you're a few feet (about 1 meter) from the takeoff. Level your pedals and coast. Stand up and pull back on the handlebars like a wheelie. In the air, shift your weight back and let the rear wheel touch first. Instantly shift your weight back. Push the front wheel down and keep it pointed forward.

Someday jumping skills will come in handy on the U-ramp. But long before you chuck yourself high off the half-pipe, and even before you drop in from the deck, you must learn to carve an arc up and down on the curved transition, or tranny, walls. Ride up too straight and you turtle backwards. Lean away from the tranny.

RAD TRIVIA

- Longest Bicycle Wheelie: In 1998, Kurt Osborn rode a wheelie for 11 hours to set a record (why else would you do it, huh?).
- Longest Backward Ride: Way back in 1897, Jacob Wainwright rode his bike backwards for 440 yards. He did it in 39 seconds (no 15 minutes of fame there).

You gain more control of your bike during races when you practice jumping.

PUMP UP THE VERT

Start pumping for speed instead of pedaling. Push and pull; bend and unbend your knees and elbows to build momentum.

If that feels good, throw in a bunny-hop at the top of your carve. Start pumping bigger and higher arcs until you can ride up onto the deck. The vertical walls look much taller and the tranny looks much steeper from up there. To come down, you can either hike your bike over the backside (and face gales of laughter for the rest of your riding lifetime) or you can ease into the ramp.

Starting a bit back from the coping, position the bike at an angle as if you've already made a huge carve and this is the last part of the arc. Hold yourself steady with your inside foot on the deck and the outside foot on the pedal. Push yourself into a slow roll up and over the coping. Lean into the ramp and away from the deck to keep from sliding. Who-yah!

TURN THIS WAY

If you're right-handed and right-footed, make counterclockwise turns. Left-handed or goofy-footed riders should carve clockwise.

WINNING ON WHEELS

Several of the original BMX motocross racecourses of the 1970s still exist. New ones popped up across America and all over the world. But even with a national racing program, many kids live too far from a course to practice regularly. They tend to make their own courses and focus on tricks.

Thanks to EXPN and its X Games, the freestyle side of BMX riding lets kids see how far they can go with the sport. Other big contests, such as the Gravity Games, the CFB (Crazy Freakin' Bikers) Series, and the Bicycle Stunt (BS) Series showcase the world's most talented riders. Many local bike shops also sponsor shows and contests, too.

chapter
FIVE

Who knows what you might do someday? Ride every type of bike. Experiment and create your own moves. Dance with your bike and make it a party on wheels. For BMX riders, it's all about having fun.

SOARING SUCCESS STORY

Name: Mat "The Condor" Hoffman
Born: 1/9/72
Height: 6' (183 cm)
Weight: 160 lbs. (72.6 kg)
Started competing: Age 13
Career Highlights:
- Invented more than 50 tricks, including the flair, Indian air and no-hands 540
- Landed the first 900
- Set the record for highest air: 26.5 feet (8.1 m) off a 24-foot (7.3 m) quarter-pipe vert ramp
- Ten-time World Champion

Mat Hoffman dares his sport to grow stale. Sixteen years after his first contest, he still pushes BMX freestyle with new tricks, new bikes and new events. Some people call him the Michael Jordan of BMX. In the year 2000 alone, he won the Bicycle Stunt (BS) Series, CFB Series, European Championship and World Championship. Not bad for a dad, huh?

Mat Hoffman soars over the crowd, always getting big air for his tricks.

Mat also runs several businesses. He started Hoffman Bikes, Hoffman Promotions, and Hoffman Sports Association—the organization that approves trick bike competitions, including the X Games events. He stars in a video game and movies, promotes the BS and CFB series, and still finds time to ride his bike.

Interestingly, the town of Edmond, Oklahoma, nearly left out BMX riders when the new skate park opened there. Oops! Fortunately, the planners remembered that one world-famous BMX athlete by the name of Mat Hoffman grew up in Edmond. They changed their rules.

SPIN FORWARD

BMX freestyle bikes show up everywhere today. You see preschoolers playing with "finger bike" toys. You also catch a few adults playing with those realistic little bikes! All kinds of computer and video games highlight the thrills and strategy of BMX tricks, too. The fad of the 1970s survived and found new life in the 1990s. Share the wheeling excitement as it spins into the next century.

FURTHER READING

Your library and the Internet can help you learn more about BMX riding. Check these titles and sites for starters:

Guinness World Records 2001. London: Guinness World Records, 2000.

Eck, Kristine, and L.M. Burke, Chris Hayhurst. *Extreme Sports Collection: Bicycle Stunt Riding!: Catch Air*. PowerKids Press, 1999

Glaser, Jason. *Extreme Sports: Bicycle Stunt Riding*. Capstone Press, 1999

Knox, Barbara. *New Action Sports: BMX Bicycles*. Capstone Press, 1996.

WEBSITES TO VISIT

www.bmxriders.org

www.expn.go.com

www.info@guinnessrecords.com

www.hsacentral.com

www.bmxfreestyleland.com

www.bmx.cc

www.BMXonline.com

www.wofbmx.com

www.woodwardcamp.com

GLOSSARY

antiseptic (an tih SEP tik) — a spray, lotion, or cream that kills germs and bacteria

calipers (KAL uh perz) — a unit with two arms on each side of the wheel that pull against the rims to slow or stop the bike

courtesy (KUR tuh see) — polite manners

disciplines (DIS uh plinz) — styles or types

emergency (ih MUR jin see) — fast medical care

fractures (FRAK cherz) — breaks or cracks in bones

independent (in dih PEN dent) — not connected to others; separate; original

intimidate (in TIM ih dayt) — scare or challenge

lubricate (LOO bra kayt) — applying a thin layer of oil over parts that rub against each other

obstacles (AHB stuh kilz) — things blocking a path; in BMX, this includes jumps, rails, or gaps

pedestrians (peh DES tree enz) — people traveling by foot, like walkers or joggers

petroleum (puh TROH lee um) — oil-based

physics (FIZ iks) — the science of matter, energy, motion, and force

precision (prih SIZH un) — exactly correct

reflectors (rih FLEK terz) — plastic disks or bars that bounce back
    light to help bikes or other objects show up in the dark

stationary (STAY shu nahr ee) — not moving, fixed

strategy (STRAT uh jee) — plan

terrain (tuh RAYN) — ground or surface; landscape

traction (TRAK shun) — gripping power

INDEX

ABOUT THE AUTHOR

Tracy Nelson Maurer specializes in nonfiction and business writing. Her most recently published children's books include the *A to Z* series, also from Rourke Publishing LLC. She lives with her husband Mike and two children in Superior, Wisconsin.